smoothies

smoothies

50 RECIPES FOR
HIGH-ENERGY REFRESHMENT

MARY CORPENING BARBER, SARA CORPENING,
AND LORI LYN NARLOCK

PHOTOGRAPHS BY AMY NEUNSINGER

CHRONICLE BOOKS
SAN FRANCISCO

Library of Congress Cataloging-in-Publication Data available.

ISBN 0-8118-1648-6

Printed in Hong Kong.

Prop and Food stylist: Carol Applegate
Designed by Elizabeth Van Itallie/Hello Studio
Photographer's assistant: Lisa Durham

Distributed in Canada by Raincoast Books
8680 Cambie Street
Vancouver, British Columbia V6P 6M9

10 9 8

Chronicle Books
85 Second Street
San Francisco, California 94105

www.chroniclebooks.com

acknowledgments

First and foremost, we want to thank our editor, Bill LeBlond, and his staff for guiding us through this adventure.

We also want to extend thanks to our friends who have tested, tasted, and shared their ideas, opinions, and assistance along the way, especially Sara Slavin, Tori Ritchie, and Jan Janek.

MARY AND SARA: We dedicate our work on this book to Mom and Dad, who have been our inspiration from day one. Our gratitude to Paul Grimes and Katherine Alford for arousing our intense curiosity in the kitchen. Our sincere thanks to Gina Zarrilli and Marcy Bassoff for believing in us. And to Erik and Jack, we are forever grateful for your undying patience and faithful support, which kept us from losing our sanity. Last but not least, we so appreciate our loyal intern, Tania, for her sense of humor and dedication throughout this project.

LORI: I dedicate my contribution to this book in loving memory to my brother Ronnie, whose voracious appetite for life was equally matched by his hunger for good food. My deepest appreciation to my grandparents and my parents for their love and support. Thank you to Eric Haven, for reading everything I have ever written; to Nancy Garfinkel, for your encouragement and confidence; and to Michael Dashe, for giving me my first writing job and teaching me how to use metaphors. I owe a debt of gratitude to my dear friend Mark Stofle, who was a brave taster early in my culinary career. And lastly to my sister, Lisa, thank you for your warm heart, kind spirit, and life-saving sense of humor.

contents

decadent medleys 70

drunken concoctions 88

intro-duction

Get your blender ready. It's smoothie time.

Easy to prepare, nourishing, and delicious blended fruit drinks, smoothies are the quintessential beverage for our fast-paced lives. Healthy and indulgent, they know no gender, age, or lifestyle limit.

The first smoothie was undoubtedly the sweet Orange Julius that we loved as kids. In the seventies it was replaced with a fruit blend that incorporated a protein powder to satisfy muscle-building enthusiasts. Now the two have converged and are proliferating in adventurous combinations of fruits, milks, sorbets, yogurts, and a variety of other binders and flavorings.

Anyone can prepare and enjoy smoothies—all you need is a knife, a blender, and a few fresh ingredients. Like magnets, smoothies attract boyfriends, wives, parents, siblings, and friends into the kitchen to share. They are so simple that parents can premeasure ingredients for children to blend later; gym rats can drink them as a power boost before a workout; and even the most sedentary can blend a batch on the way to the couch. Once prepared, smoothies are perfect for drinking in the kitchen, on the playing field, at the office, or in the car.

And smoothie time is anytime. We guzzle them in the morning, sip them after lunch, swill them for dessert, and tipple them before bed. They are an energy boost, a healthy snack, a hangover helper, a quick breakfast, a lazy dinner, and a refreshing thirst quencher.

Dairy-lovers, tofu-zealots, and caffeine-nuts will all discover a favorite smoothie recipe within these pages. This book represents our favorite recipes derived from many hours of blending and tasting. The chapters in this book are divided by the type of binder that is used in the smoothie. Wholesome Mergers use fruit juice and yogurt as a binder; No-Moo Blends incorporate sorbet, tofu, soy milk, and rice milk into fresh fruit; Decadent Medleys combine frozen yogurt with fruit; and Drunken Concoctions are all of the above with the addition of alcohol.

So, turn to any recipe that captures your attention and start your blender!

nutritional information

Smoothies are a healthy food choice. They incorporate a variety of fruits and binders that provide essential nutrients in the form of a deliciously indulgent drink. Building smoothies into a diet helps to meet the daily recommendations set by the United States Department of Agriculture.

In 1992, the USDA created a food guide for consumers in the shape of a pyramid that outlines the components of a healthy diet. The middle of the pyramid consists of fruit, dairy, and protein food groups: all the ingredients used to make smoothies. As part of a 2,000-calorie diet, recommended for most children, teenagers, active women, and sedentary men, smoothies can help to supply the following recommended daily foods: 3 to 4 half-cup servings of raw fruit; 2 to 3 one-cup servings of dairy products such as milk or yogurt; 2 to 3 two-tablespoon to half-cup servings of nuts and beans, such as ½ cup tofu or 2 tablespoons peanut butter.

Along with the food pyramid guide, the USDA has created a guideline for how much of any one type of nutrient is needed to maintain a healthy and well-functioning body. A 2,000-calorie diet should supply but not exceed these amounts: total fat 65 g; cholesterol 300 mg; carbohydrates 300 g; dietary fiber 25 g; sodium 2,400 mg; potassium 300 mg; calcium 1,200 mg; iron 20 mg; vitamin A 5,000 i.u.; vitamin C 60 mg.

The consumption of any type of food results in the intake of calories. Calories are the measurement of a single energy unit, and calorie content is determined by the type of food: 1 gram of fat has 9 calories, 1 gram of protein has 4 calories, and carbohydrates also have 4 calories for every gram. Many smoothies are high in calories because fruit is naturally high in carbohydrates. Calories that are derived from carbohydrates are easier to burn off and harder to convert to body fat, unlike calories from fat.

Although fat is an essential nutrient for maintaining a healthy body, a smart diet should not contain more than 20 to 30 percent fat. Because the primary ingredient of a smoothie is fruit, most smoothies are very low in fat. Most of the recipes in this book contain fewer than 3 grams of fat per 12-fluid-ounce serving. This is considered low fat by the Food and Drug Administration standards.

Most smoothies are low in cholesterol. There are two types of cholesterol: a good type that can be increased through exercise and a bad type that can build up in the arteries and lead to heart disease. The bad type of cholesterol can be kept to a minimum through a careful diet that is high in fiber. Fruits—particularly those with edible skin and seeds, such as kiwis, apples, blueberries, raspberries, and plums—are a great source of fiber.

Fruit is also an important source of carbohydrates, which are easily converted into energy and also create a "full" feeling when consumed. Because smoothies are packed with carbohydrates, they're perfect for a filling meal or energy boost.

In addition to fruit, smoothies also contain a binder. Some of the smoothies in this book have a fruit-based binder such as juice or sorbet, while others contain a dairy product, nut butter, or nondairy ingredient such as tofu. These binders are included because they are an important source of protein, which helps to maintain healthy muscles, bones, skin, and internal organs. Because protein can be found in a wide variety of foods, most Americans get all the protein they need through their diet. Excess protein through supplements is usually unnecessary.

Smoothies are a good source of minerals, which help regulate a body's balance of water, hormones, enzymes, vitamins, and fluids. The most prominent minerals in smoothies are sodium, potassium, calcium, and iron.

SODIUM is essential to our bodies primarily for maintaining a proper amount of body fluids. But we need far less than what most of us consume daily. Fruit is generally low in sodium, so drinking smoothies that contain only fruit may help to lower your sodium intake.

POTASSIUM is essential for lowering blood pressure and keeping muscles strong and healthy. Bananas (one of the most common smoothie ingredients), along with many other fruits, are a good source of potassium.

CALCIUM promotes healthy bones and is especially important for preventing osteoporosis in women. Smoothies that have milk, yogurt, frozen yogurt, and calcium-fortified or -enriched soy milk, rice milk, or tofu provide calcium.

IRON, which carries oxygen to the blood, is most easily absorbed when it is consumed in combination with vitamin C. Smoothies that combine citrus with tofu and/or soy milk will help to provide an iron-rich diet.

Smoothies are also a great source of vitamins A and C.

VITAMIN A is beneficial for the immune system and eyes as well as other functions. When consumed in the form of beta carotene, it is an important antioxidant that helps to prevent cancer. Bright-colored fruits such as apricots, mangoes, cherries, and cantaloupes contain high levels of beta carotene.

VITAMIN C, the other prominent antioxidant, is abundant in citrus, kiwi, strawberries, and cranberries. Vitamin C also plays an important role in preventing infections, assisting healing, and growing healthy teeth, bones, and gums.

In addition to the natural health benefits of smoothies, nutritional supplements can be added to any recipe. Many additives can be purchased at a natural food store or pharmacy in powder or liquid form. Although nutritional supplements have long been believed to provide health benefits, most are not scientifically proven. Some common supplements follow:

GINSENG Contains a stimulant similar to caffeine
GOTU KOLA Contains vitamins A, C, and K as well as magnesium
BRAN Provides dietary fiber
SOYBEAN POWDER Contains a concentrated amount of protein
BEE POLLEN Provides an abundance of necessary nutrients
SPIRULINA Provides protein, minerals, and vitamins
GINKGO BILOBA An antioxidant
BREWER'S YEAST Contains an abundance of B vitamins
WHEAT GERM Contains vitamin E, protein, and iron

Nutritionists agree that the best way to stay healthy is to eat a balanced diet. A smoothie with fresh fruit and a nutritious binder is a good step towards that. If you think you have a dietary deficiency, visit with a nutritionally minded health provider to determine the best supplement for your needs. Before adding any supplement to your smoothie, be aware that it may change the taste and texture of your smoothie—you might not want to drink a smoothie that tastes like the bottom of the ocean!

The Nutritional Analyses chapter lists nutrient values for each recipe. The nutritional information is based on one 12-fluid-ounce serving. The actual nutrient content of your smoothie may vary slightly, depending on the brands of ingredients used.

For more nutritional information, call the American Dietetic Association Nutrition Hotline at (800) 366-1655. Recorded messages are available 8 AM to 8 PM and registered dietitians are available 9 AM to 4 PM.

perfect fruit

selecting, preparing, and storing fresh fruit

Succulent peaches. Buttery pears. Juicy berries. Descriptions of fruit alone are enough to start your mouth watering. Now, imagine frosty blends that capture the essence of a single fruit or a combination of complementary fruits—that is what smoothies are all about.

Finding and preparing the best fruit is the most important step towards making the best smoothie. The freshest-tasting smoothies are those made with tree-ripened fruit at the peak of its season. This means fruit that has been allowed to fully mature on the tree before being picked and that isn't the first of the season or the last. Many types of fruit can become ripe off the tree, but their sugar content—and sweetness—will not be as high as in fruit left to ripen on the tree. Often, fruit is picked early in order to be shipped. And some fruits, such as apples, are sometimes stored during their off season for availability later. In both these situations, the fruit may lack full flavor. To avoid bland fruit, buy fruit when it is in season and grown locally—ask your grocer which fruit is from nearby farms. Or, buy directly from the grower at a farmers' market whenever possible. Organic fruit, which is becoming more widely available, is also a smart choice because of its lack of pesticides.

Don't despair when fresh fruit isn't available. Many types of fruit are available packaged frozen. Fruit that is available frozen is usually fruit with the shortest growing season, such as berries and peaches. Some packaged frozen fruit, such as raspberries, boysenberries, and cranberries, is often more economical than fresh and just as flavorful. Organic fruit is also available packaged frozen. When using frozen fruit, buy unsweetened packages, not fruit that is frozen in a sugar syrup.

Whenever possible, buy fruit that is already ripe. (Bananas and pears usually must be ripened at home.) If you must ripen fruit, simply let it sit at room temperature for several days. To accelerate the ripening process, place the fruit in a plastic or paper bag with bananas and test the fruit daily for signs of ripeness. During warmer seasons, watch fruit more closely, because it will ripen faster. Never refrigerate unripe fruit.

Use these guidelines to select perfect fruit:

- **UNRIPE FRUIT** is hard, green, and scentless. When you bite into it, you want to just spit it right back out.
- **SLIGHTLY UNRIPE** One or more signs of ripeness exist, but the smell and taste are bland. If you close your eyes, you might not be able to determine what you are eating.
- **PERFECT** The fruit shows all signs of ripeness—sight, smell, and touch. It's green only if it's a lime; when you lift it to your nose its perfume is intense; and when you squeeze it in your palm it feels tender, like an extra-firm foam mattress, not hard like a golf ball.
- **OVERLY RIPE** The fruit has soft spots, bruises, or mold. (Otherwise known as a day late and a dollar short.)

Most of the recipes in this book call for fresh fruit that is frozen at home. Most fruit will reach a firmly frozen stage in 2 to 4 hours, depending on the fruit and the temperature of your freezer. For maximum flavor, we suggest that you use fruit within 1 to 2 weeks of freezing it. Store-bought frozen fruit can last longer, because it is frozen immediately after being picked instead of sitting in a store or in your home. We recommend that you use packaged frozen fruit within 6 months of purchase or within 2 weeks after opening.

Not all of the fruit used in our recipes is frozen. And for any fruit that is called for frozen, nonfrozen fresh can be substituted. If you prefer to use fresh fruit, add ice cubes to your smoothie until the desired consistency and temperature is reached.

To freeze fresh fruit, dice it finely, then freeze it lying flat in a self-sealing plastic bag. This not only makes it easy to measure it frozen, it also saves freezer space. Be sure to dry any fruit that is washed before freezing by patting it dry with paper towels. For fragile fruit, such as berries, lay washed berries flat on paper towels to remove excess water.

For the sake of convenience, buy a week's worth of fruit at a time, then peel, dice, and store it at once. If you have small amounts of fruit left over at the end of 2 weeks, make a "leftover" smoothie by blending it with juice and adding yogurt until it reaches a desired consistency.

Prepare ingredients for several smoothies at one time and use them throughout the week.

fruit glossary

This glossary describes each of the fruits used in this book and lists the peak season, gives instructions on how to prepare the fruit for a smoothie, and when applicable tells how to ripen at home.

APPLES

The best apples for smoothies are crisp, tart varieties such as a green Granny Smith, a yellow Golden Delicious, or a red Braeburn or Gala. Always select apples that have smooth, unbruised, and blemish-free skins. Although apples are available year-round, they are at their peak from September through November.

PREPARATION: Peel, core, and halve. Lay flat-side down and cut into ½-inch dice. Place in a plastic bag and freeze until firm. Prep time for 1 pound: 5 to 10 minutes. Yield: 3 to 4 cups diced fruit.

APRICOTS

Apricots are available beginning in May, but the late-harvest fruit in June and July is usually sweeter. Select apricots that are plump, pliable, and uniformly colored. The sweeter the apricot, the more perfume it will have—a good indication that it will have a nice creamy texture. Once picked, apricots won't become sweeter.

PREPARATION: Halve and pit. Lay flat-side down and cut into ½-inch dice. Place in a plastic bag and freeze until firm. Prep time for 1 pound: 4 to 7 minutes. Yield: approximately 2 cups diced fruit.

BANANAS

The yellow Cavendish is the most commonly eaten banana. Available year-round, bananas are always in season. Buy bananas in any stage of ripeness and let unripe fruit sit out at room temperature until it begins to develop brown spots and become fragrant.

PREPARATION: Freeze several bananas at one time for quick use later. Peel, place in a plastic bag, and freeze. Slice when ready to use. Prep time for 1 pound: 2 to 3 minutes.

BLACKBERRIES

Blackberries are at their peak during July and August. Select berries that are plump, firm, uniformly deep colored, and mold free. Avoid berries with the hulls attached; this is an indication that they were picked too early and will be tart.

PREPARATION: Sort through the berries and discard any that are moldy or spoiled. Place in a plastic bag and freeze until firm. Prep time for 1 pint: 2 to 3 minutes. Yield: approximately 2 cups whole fruit.

BLUEBERRIES

These sweet and juicy dark blue berries are available year-round, with a peak season of June through September. Select berries that are plump, firm, uniformly colored, and mold free.

PREPARATION: Sort through the berries and discard any that are moldy or spoiled. Remove any stems. Place in a plastic bag and freeze until firm. Prep time for 1 pint: 2 to 3 minutes. Yield: approximately 2 cups whole fruit.

BOYSENBERRIES

The boysenberry looks like an oversized, deep red and purple raspberry and has a sweet-tart taste. Select berries that are plump, firm, uniformly colored, and mold free. Avoid berries with the hulls attached; this is an indication that they were picked too early and will be tart. Boysenberries generally have a short season—only July.

PREPARATION: Sort through berries and discard any that are moldy or spoiled. Place in a plastic bag and freeze until firm. Prep time for 1 pint: 2 to 3 minutes. Yield: approximately 2 cups whole fruit.

CANTALOUPES

A perfectly ripened melon will have a pronounced, uniform orange tone under the netting of the skin and the blossom end will be tender when pressed with a thumb. The sweetest melons exude a definite perfume. Select melons that are heavy for their size. Cantaloupes are available year-round, with a peak season of June through September.

PREPARATION: Slice off both ends. Place one end down on a cutting surface and cut along the sides, from top to bottom, to remove the rind. Halve and remove the seeds with a spoon. Cut the flesh into ½-inch dice. Store in a sealed plastic container or bag in the refrigerator until ready to use. Prep time for one 2-pound melon: 5 to 7 minutes. Yield: approximately 4 cups diced fruit.

CHERRIES

At the peak of their season, June through August, cherries are plump, sweet, and juicy. Always buy cherries that are glossy, evenly colored, and tender when pressed between your fingers. Those with stems attached are best; always avoid bruised or soft fruit. Once picked, cherries won't become sweeter.

PREPARATION: Halve; remove the pit with your fingertips or a small knife. Place in a plastic bag and freeze until firm. Prep time for 1 pound:

12 to 15 minutes. Yield: approximately 2½ cups halved fruit.

COCONUTS

The coconut has a white lining inside the shell that is sweet and delicious. Fresh coconuts are usually available year-round, although their peak season is October through December. Buy coconuts that have dry eyes on the exterior and liquid in the center (shake them to check).

PREPARATION: Fresh coconut is a delicious addition to smoothies, but the most convenient and practical way to include the taste of coconut is to use coconut milk, extract, or store-bought shredded coconut. To prepare a fresh coconut, use a heavy hammer to bust open the shell. Use a spoon to separate fruit from shell. Grate fruit using the small holes of a hand grater. Store in a sealed container. Prep time for a 1-pound coconut: 8 to 10 minutes. Yield: approximately 1 cup shredded fruit.

CRANBERRIES

These small crimson-red berries have a tart and acidic taste and are available October through December. Buy berries that are plump and already ripe.

PREPARATION: Test cranberries for freshness by floating them in a bowl of water; discard any berries that sink or are soft. Place in a plastic bag and freeze. Prep time for one 12-ounce bag: 2 to 3 minutes. Yield: approximately 2 cups whole fruit.

DATES

Fresh dates are sweet, chewy, and sticky. Select those that are plump, 1 to 2 inches long, and have skin that is uniformly colored golden to dark brown. Store dates in a sealed container or plastic bag in a cool, dark place.

PREPARATION: Halve, pit, and chop. To prevent the dates from sticking to the knife, dip the blade in hot water. Prep time for 1 pound: 10 to 12 minutes. Yield: approximately 2 cups chopped fruit.

GRAPES

Choose seedless grapes for smoothies. Green grapes are usually the sweetest, but red and purple grapes are quite sweet, although their skins may impart a bitter taste. Buy plump, smooth-skinned grapes firmly attached to the stem and in nice clusters. Grapes are available year-round, although each variety has a peak season; the sweetest varieties are ripe August through September.

PREPARATION: Separate grapes from the stems, place in a plastic bag and freeze until firm. Prep time for 1 pound: 3 to 5 minutes. Yield: approximately 2 cups whole fruit.

GRAPEFRUITS

Available year-round, grapefruits range in skin and flesh color from pale yellow to deep pink. Their sweetness varies from cloying to mouth-puckeringly sour. Select grapefruits that are heavy for their size.

PREPARATION: Cut a slice off both ends down to the flesh. Set one end on a cutting surface. Cut away the peel, down to the flesh, from top to bottom. Using a very sharp knife, cut the segments out of the membrane that holds them (it can be very bitter). Place the segments in a plastic bag and freeze until firm. Prep time for 1 pound: 8 to 10 minutes. Yield: approximately 1 cup fruit segments.

GUAVAS

These tropical fruits are grown in California, Hawaii, and Florida. They have a smooth dark green skin and are oval shaped. Small seeds are enclosed in their yellow to white flesh. Most commercially available fruit is imported from New Zealand, so its peak season is October through January.

PREPARATION: It is often difficult to find guavas, so we use nectar in place of the fruit. Guava nectar is readily available in grocery stores. For fresh guavas, peel, halve, remove seeds, and dice fruit. Place in a plastic bag and freeze until firm. Prep time for 1 guava: 3 to 5 minutes. Yield: approximately 1 cup diced fruit.

HONEYDEWS

A member of the muskmelon family, the green-fleshed, sweet honeydew is available year-round, but is at its peak season from July through August. Select melons that are shiny, pale yellow to green, and heavy for their size. A ripe melon will have a nice perfume and small wrinkles can be felt with your hands but not seen.

PREPARATION: Slice off both ends. Place one end down on a cutting surface and cut along the sides, from top to bottom, to remove the rind. Halve and remove the seeds with a spoon. Cut the flesh into ½-inch dice. Store in a sealed plastic container or bag in the refrigerator until ready to use. Prep time for one 6-pound melon: 5 to 7 minutes. Yield: 5 to 6 cups diced fruit.

KIWIS

The fuzzy brown egg-shaped kiwi exterior hides a sweet-tart fruit that is speckled with little black seeds. Kiwis are available year-round. Select kiwis that are tender when squeezed in your palm.

PREPARATION: Using a sharp paring knife, slice off both ends and cut away the peel by cutting in strips from one end to the other. Cut into a fine dice. Store in a sealed plastic container or bag in the refrigerator until ready to use. Prep time for 1 pound of kiwi: 8 to 12 minutes. Yield: approximately 1 cup diced fruit.

LEMONS

The tart acidic taste of lemons helps to balance the sweetness of some smoothies. Select lemons that are heavy for their size and feel tender when squeezed in your palm. They will be juicier. The vitamin C in lemon juice begins to dissipate from oxidation after being squeezed, so don't prepare lemons until ready to use. Like most citrus, lemons don't like hot weather, so they peak in the fall and winter.

PREPARATION: To get the most juice from a lemon, before squeezing put it in the microwave for 10 seconds or roll it around on a counter top applying pressure with your palm. Halve and squeeze using a juicer. If you don't have a juicer, squeeze in the palm of your hand. Prep time for 1 lemon: 2 minutes. Yield: 2 to 3 tablespoons juice.

LIMES

Limes have a sour taste that is a wonderful complement to all kinds of foods. Select limes that are heavy for their size, thin skinned, and plump. Limes are available year-round, but they are most prolific from May through August.

PREPARATION: Cut a slice off both ends down to the flesh. Set one end on a cutting surface. Cut away the peel, down to the flesh, from top to bottom. Using a very sharp knife, cut the segments out of the membrane that holds them (it can be very bitter). Place the segments in a plastic bag and freeze until firm. Prep time for 5 limes: 12 to 15 minutes. Yield: approximately 1 cup fruit segments.

MANGOES

The best mangoes are those that have ripened to a bright yellow or orange with red tones. Green mangoes will ripen and become sweet, but have a less robust flavor. Mangoes are round to kidney shaped and have a sweet and creamy interior. Select mangoes that are tender when squeezed and have a sweet aroma. Mangoes are available year-round, with a peak season of April through July.

PREPARATION: Peel, slice the fruit away from the long seed, and dice. Place in a plastic bag and freeze until firm. Prep time for 1 medium mango: 5 minutes. Yield: approximately 1½ cups diced fruit.

NECTARINES

A smooth-skinned cousin to the peach, nectarines are juicy and buttery. Their orange skin blushes with red highlights, and their ripeness can be judged by aroma and touch—they should be tender when gently squeezed in your palm. Buy nectarines during their peak season from June through August.

PREPARATION: Halve, remove the pit with a spoon (not a knife), and cut the fruit into ½-inch dice. Place in a plastic bag and freeze until firm. Prep time for 1 pound: 5 to 7 minutes. Yield: approximately 1½ cups diced fruit.

ORANGES

For the best smoothie, use a seedless orange variety, such as navel in winter or Valencia in the spring and summer. Because the color of an orange does not reveal its ripeness, you should select oranges that are heavy for their size and avoid any with soft or spongy spots or blemishes. Oranges are available year-round, although different varieties have different peak seasons. Blood oranges, a unique hybrid that have a tart berry flavor and a deep-red flesh, are ripest December through February.

PREPARATION: Cut a slice off both ends down to the flesh. Set one end on a cutting surface. Cut away the peel, down to the flesh, from top to bottom. Using a very sharp knife, cut the segments out of the membrane that holds them (it can be very bitter). Place the segments in a plastic bag and freeze until firm. Prep time for 1 pound: 10 to 12 minutes. Yield: approximately 1½ cups fruit segments.

PAPAYAS

There are several types of papaya available, including Mexican, strawberry, and the most common type, Solo. Because they are grown in year-round warm-climate areas, they are available throughout the year, but peak in early summer. The Solo variety has a greenish-gold exterior and a bright salmon-pink fruit with a subtle, sweet taste. Ripe papayas are tender and may have a mottled or spotty exterior. Papayas are respected for their digestive assisting qualities and are a good source of vitamins A and C.

PREPARATION: Halve, remove the seeds with a spoon, peel, and cut into ½-inch dice. Place in a plastic bag and freeze until firm. Prep time for a 1-pound papaya: 4 to 6 minutes. Yield: approximately 1½ cups diced fruit.

PASSION FRUITS

The exterior of the passion fruit looks dried up and wrinkled when it hits its peak of ripeness. Lying beneath the shriveled skin is a chartreuse flesh with yellow-green seeds and a bright pink magenta lining. Passion fruit is available year-round, but on a limited basis.

PREPARATION: Because they aren't always easy to find and their yield is very small, we use passion fruit juice and sorbet as smoothie ingredients. For fresh passion fruit, cut in half and scoop out fruit. Strain through a sieve to remove seeds or use pulp and seeds. Place in a sealed container and refrigerate or freeze until ready to use. Prep time for 1 passion fruit: 3 to 5 minutes. Yield: 1 to 2 tablespoons juice.

PEACHES

There are more than two thousand peach hybrids, ranging in skin color from white to deep orange with red tones. The fruit's interior also ranges in color and taste, from deliciously sweet, firm white fruit to juicy, slightly tart orange flesh. Peaches are at their peak from June to July and should be purchased as close to ripe as possible, because once they've been picked they don't become sweeter. Select peaches that are free from blemishes and bruises, have a sweet perfume, and are tender when squeezed.

PREPARATION: Peel, halve, remove the pit with a spoon (not a knife), and cut into ½-inch dice. Place in a plastic bag and freeze until firm. Prep time for 1 pound: 5 to 7 minutes. Yield: approximately 2 cups diced fruit.

PEARS

For smoothies, use buttery pears such as Bartletts in summer and Comices in winter. The distinctive taste of a pear improves as it ripens and becomes more creamy. A ripe pear will have a marked scent and will be tender when pressed at the stem end. Pears bruise easily and should be handled with care.

PREPARATION: Using a sharp knife, peel. Cut into quarters, core, and cut into ½-inch dice. Place in a plastic bag and freeze until firm. Prep time for 1 pound: 10 to 12 minutes. Yield: approximately 2 cups diced fruit.

PINEAPPLES

Select pineapples with a nicely raised diamond texture that is bright yellow beneath the scales, crisp green leaves, and a sweet aroma. For pineapples that aren't completely ripe, cut off leaves to make a flat surface and turn upside down in a warm place to evenly distribute the sugar. The result will be a juicy, sweet, and slightly tart center. Pineapples are available year-round.

PREPARATION: Slice off the top and the bottom. Set one end on a flat cutting surface and cut along the sides, from top to bottom, removing all of the outer peel. Cut into quarters, cut away core, and chop into ½-inch dice. Place in a plastic bag, and freeze until firm. Prep time for one 4-pound pineapple: 12 to 15 minutes. Yield: 3 to 4 cups diced fruit.

PLUMS

Plums are available May through October, with different varieties ranging in color and sweetness. Once picked, plums don't become sweeter. Buy aromatic, plump plums that are firm but pliable when squeezed. The skin may be sour, but a ripe plum will have a sweet and juicy center.

PREPARATION: Halve and pit. If the skin is sour, peel. Cut into ½-inch dice, place in a plastic bag and freeze until firm. Prep time for 1 pound: 6 to 8 minutes. Yield: approximately 2 cups diced fruit.

RASPBERRIES

Whether golden or red, raspberries are sweet and delicious. The peak season for fresh raspberries is May through September. Imported raspberries are sometimes available throughout the year.

PREPARATION: Sort through berries and discard any that are moldy or spoiled. Place in a plastic bag and freeze until firm. Prep time for 1 pint: 2 to 3 minutes. Yield: approximately 1½ cups whole fruit.

RHUBARB

There are two types of rhubarb, hothouse and field. The first is available year-round, and the second is available in spring. The large pink to magenta stalks should be brightly colored and show no pith (stringiness) or decay on the ends.

PREPARATION: Raw rhubarb is bitter and fibrous, so it must be cooked. Slice first and then dice to reduce stringiness. Refrigerate until ready to cook (see page 43). Prep time for 1 pound: 4 to 6 minutes. Yield: approximately 3 cups diced fruit.

STRAWBERRIES

A sweet aroma is the best indication of a ripe strawberry. Avoid berries that are bruised, moldy, or have white shoulders. Strawberries are often available year-round, with a peak season from April to June.

PREPARATION: Remove the hull using the tip of a vegetable peeler or a sharp paring knife. Cut into quarters, place in a plastic bag and freeze until firm. Prep time for 1 pint: 6 to 8 minutes. Yield: approximately 2 cups quartered fruit.

WATERMELONS

This cool, refreshing, and oh-so-tasty melon is available with red and yellow flesh, with or without seeds. Select watermelons that make a hollow sound when thumped and are heavy for their size. The rind should be dull, not shiny, and have a light spot on the bottom. Avoid melons with cracks or blemishes. Watermelons have a peak season from May to August.

PREPARATION: Cut into quarters. If the melon has seeds, cut out core where most of the seeds are located. Remove all other seeds and cut the flesh into ½-inch dice. Store in sealed plastic container or bag in the refrigerator until ready to use. Prep time for one 10-pound melon: 12 to 16 minutes. Yield: approximately 16 cups diced fruit.

the ultimate smoothie

non-fruit ingredients, equipment, and techniques

Smoothies require few ingredients and even less equipment. They are so simple to prepare, anyone can make them; with a little preparation and know-how, they can be made in a matter of minutes.

non-fruit ingredients

A handful of ingredients is all it takes to make the best smoothie you've ever tasted. Smoothies are by definition a blended fruit drink, but they can be enhanced with the addition of dairy and nondairy ingredients, including nectars, extracts, and nut butters. The recipes in this book include ingredients that are readily available in most supermarkets.

If you can't find or don't particularly like a specific ingredient, feel free to substitute an ingredient that is similar in texture or taste. Following is a list of non-fruit ingredients that are used in the recipes in this book.

BUTTERMILK
Originally the milk that remained when butter was churned, today buttermilk is nonfat or low-fat milk that has had bacteria added to make it thick and tangy. Buttermilk has the same fat content as regular yogurt, about 2 to 3 fat grams per 8-ounce serving. Because it is a fresh product, it needs to be refrigerated, but it has a longer shelf life than regular milk.

COCONUT MILK
Coconut milk is not the liquid from the center of the fruit, but is made from a mixture of water and fresh coconut meat that is boiled and then strained. Coconut milk is high in both calories and fat, but light coconut milk, which contains as much as 60 percent less fat, is also available. Unopened canned coconut milk has a long shelf life. Once opened, it can be refrigerated for up to one week.

EXTRACTS

Extracts are concentrated flavorings captured from a plant through a distillation or infusion process. They are available in a wide range of flavors, from vanilla to lemon. Extracts contain a small percentage of alcohol, possess an intense flavor, and have a shelf life of many years.

FROZEN YOGURT

Frozen yogurt is a cultured dairy product that is frozen. It is available in just about every imaginable flavor and in regular and nonfat versions. It provides calcium, but most of the beneficial nutrients found in regular yogurt are dissipated once frozen. If your freezer is really cold, you may need to temper (soften) the yogurt before adding it to a smoothie. You can do this by putting it in the microwave for 10 seconds at a time or by letting it sit at room temperature for 10 to 15 minutes. Alas, not all frozen yogurts are alike; some have higher air content and result in varying smoothie yields.

JUICE

From orange to cranberry, juices are the perfect smoothie ingredient. You can squeeze your own for maximum flavor or use a concentrate mixed with water for convenience. When buying ready-made juices, check the actual fruit juice content because many can contain as little as 10 percent real juice, the rest being a variety of additives.

KEFIR

Kefir was originally made of camel's milk, and because it was believed to ensure a long healthy life, it was kept a secret from Western civilization for centuries. Today it is a fermented cow's milk and is similar to yogurt in taste. It is thicker than milk and available in plain and a few fruit flavors. It is high in phosphorous, calcium, and protein. Kefir has the same amount of fat as whole milk, about 5 fat grams per 8 ounces.

NECTAR

Nectar is made from a concentrate of pureed whole fruit. The concentrate is mixed with water and usually sweetened with corn syrup. Because of the corn syrup, nectars are high in sugar content and calories, but they contain no fat. Many types of fruit that are not readily available in juice form, such as mango, guava, and banana, are made into nectars.

PEANUT BUTTER

See Tahini and Nut Butters.

RICE MILK

Rice milk is a nondairy liquid made from organically grown brown rice that is partially milled, then cooked and pressed. It is low in fat and available in several flavors, including vanilla, chocolate, and carob. Enriched versions are available, with vitamin A, vitamin D, and calcium contents similar to that of whole milk. Unopened rice milk can be stored at room temperature for long periods of time. Once opened, it should be refrigerated for up to one week.

SHERBET

The precursor to frozen yogurt, sherbet is a low-fat version of ice cream, but the flavor range is limited to a few fruit flavors. The fat content and calories are about the same as in regular frozen yogurt, about 2 to 3 fat grams per half-cup. If your freezer is really cold, you may need to soften sherbet before adding it to a smoothie. You can do this by putting it in the microwave for 10 seconds at a time or by letting it sit at room temperature for 10 to 15 minutes.

SORBET

Sorbet is a fruit puree or essence of a food that is sweetened and then frozen. It is available in a wide range of flavors, from chocolate to passion fruit. It is dairy free and fat free. If your freezer is really cold, you may need to soften sorbet before adding it to a smoothie. You can do this by putting it in the microwave for 10 seconds at a time or by letting it sit at room temperature for 10 to 15 minutes.

SOY MILK

Soy milk is a protein- and iron-rich nondairy liquid made by pressing cooked soybeans. Most brands offer a spectrum of flavors and are calcium fortified, cholesterol free, and low in fat and sodium. Unopened soy milk can be stored at room temperature for long periods of time. Once opened, it can be refrigerated for up to one week.

TAHINI AND NUT BUTTERS

Made from sesame seeds, tahini paste has a distinctive nutty taste. Peanut butter is the most common ground nut butter, but pistachio and almond butters are gaining in popularity. Tahini and nut butters are high in protein but also high in fat, so they should be used in small amounts. Keep refrigerated or store in a cool, dark place.

TOFU

Tofu, made by curdling soy milk, is a good source of protein and iron. The best tofu for smoothies is soft silken tofu, which is slightly more creamy than soft tofu. Soft silken tofu is often sold in a small cardboard box found in the refrigerator section of the supermarket or in the Asian ingredients aisle. If purchased already cold, refrigerate until ready to use; otherwise, store in a cool, dark place.

YOGURT

This cultured dairy product is available in regular, low-fat, and nonfat varieties, and flavors range from fruit to coffee. Yogurt's bacteria is very beneficial to good health. Smoothies made with yogurt will separate, and should be served immediately.

equipment

Smoothies require a minimum amount of equipment: a knife, a cutting surface, measuring cups and spoons, and a blender. Self-sealing plastic bags are handy for freezing fruit and storing extra smoothies. Straws are great for drinking smoothies.

To cut fruit, always use a sharp knife and cut away from your hands and body. Most fruit preparation can be handled by a chef's knife, but use the size of knife that feels most comfortable.

Use a clean cutting surface. Most fruit is porous and will absorb the taste and smell of more aromatic foods; therefore, if you slice fruit on the same board that you just chopped an onion on, your smoothie will taste like onion. If you have only one cutting board, clean it with lemon juice to erase strong smells.

Use a spoon to remove seeds and pits and for stirring. Use a long handled spoon if it's necessary to stir a mixture when blending. Be careful not to let the spoon come into contact with the blades.

And to borrow a cliché, not all blenders are created equal. High-quality blenders will make smoothies quickly and effortlessly. Blenders that are older or of lesser quality will take more time and effort. Be patient. If you don't have a blender, use a food processor.

We freeze fruit and smoothies in self-sealing bags that can be washed and reused. You can also use any type of plastic bag or containers, but self-sealing plastic bags make it easier to lay the fruit flat for easy storage.

techniques

Buy fruit, cut fruit, blend fruit. It is that simple. The average smoothie takes 12 minutes or less to prepare.

For the best smoothies, use fresh fruit that is frozen. The results are thicker and colder without diluting the taste of the fruit with the addition of ice. Before freezing the fruit, always peel, chop, dice, and so on, according to the directions given in the Perfect Fruit chapter. Break off the amount you need and return the rest to the freezer; don't let it thaw!

Always add ingredients to the blender beginning with liquids and ending with solids, unless otherwise specified. If your blender has varying speeds, start on low speed to chop and then finish on high speed to blend completely. Once you begin to blend, if the mixture is too thick and the blender becomes stuck, turn it off. Stir from the bottom up with a long spoon, then turn the blender back on. If you need to stir while the blender is running, stir only around the top. Do not stick the spoon down into the blades.

Fruit is a variable ingredient, and the consistency of smoothies will vary as a result. If your smoothie is too thick, add more liquid, ¼ cup at a time. If it is too thin, add ice cubes one at a time until the desired consistency is reached. Or, use crushed ice for easier blending. To crush ice, place ice cubes in a thick plastic bag or inside a folded clean dish towel and pound with a rolling pin or heavy saucepan.

Premeasure the frozen ingredients for one recipe and label for quick use later.

Wholesome mergers are just that—nourishing combinations of exuberantly fresh fruit with fruit juice or yogurt. We start our day with these smoothies, indulge in them before we head out for a run or bike ride, and rely on them for a quick and healthy pick-me-up anytime. These are brilliant blends to be relished and enjoyed down to the last sip. Whether you love the tried-and-true blends such as SMOOTHIE CLASSICO or have an adventurous palate that thrives on the new smoothie combinations found in MAPLE BLUE or PLUM REGULAR, you'll find a smoothie to fit your taste in this section.

wholesome mergers

smoothie classico

This could be the granddaddy of all smoothies. Revered for its taste, simplicity, and vitamin C and potassium content, it's no wonder this is still a favorite of smoothie aficionados. Make it part of your life.

1 CUP ORANGE JUICE

1 CUP HULLED AND QUARTERED FRESH STRAWBERRIES, FROZEN (SEE PAGE 22)

2 FRESH BANANAS, FROZEN AND SLICED (SEE PAGE 15)

Pour the orange juice into a blender. Add the strawberries and bananas. Blend until smooth.

SERVES 2

* Without a doubt the most popular berry, strawberries are a member of the rose family.

dangerously red

Take a sip, close your eyes, and you'll be on your way to strawberry milkshake heaven—until the taste of raspberries hits you and you realize a strawberry milkshake could never be this good or this healthy. This slightly tart and very pink smoothie provides one and a half times the recommended daily allowance of vitamin C.

1 CUP LOW-FAT STRAWBERRY YOGURT

$1/2$ CUP CRANBERRY JUICE

$1^1/2$ CUPS HULLED AND QUARTERED FRESH STRAWBERRIES, FROZEN (SEE PAGE 22)

1 CUP FRESH RASPBERRIES, FROZEN (SEE PAGE 22)

Combine the yogurt and cranberry juice in a blender. Add the strawberries and raspberries; blend until smooth.

SERVES 2

passion!

The combination of sweet pineapple and slightly tart passion fruit is intensified by the tangy taste of kefir in this smoothie. It is a perfect antidote to a blah day; sip it morning, noon, or night.

¾ CUP PLAIN KEFIR OR PLAIN LOW-FAT YOGURT
½ CUP PASSION FRUIT NECTAR OR JUICE
1½ CUPS FRESH DICED PINEAPPLE, FROZEN
 (SEE PAGE 21)
¾ CUP PASSION FRUIT SORBET

Pour the kefir and nectar into a blender. Add the pineapple and sorbet. Blend until smooth.

SERVES 2

guava gulp

On a trip to Hawaii, Sara fell in love with guavas. Now she makes this smoothie and hangs ten at home. It has a beautiful golden color that invites you to take a drink.

1¼ CUPS GUAVA NECTAR
2 TEASPOONS FRESH LIME JUICE
2 CUPS DICED FRESH MANGO, FROZEN (SEE PAGE 19)
1 FRESH BANANA, FROZEN AND SLICED (SEE PAGE 15)

Pour the nectar and lime juice into a blender. Add the mango and banana and blend until smooth.

SERVES 2

peachy keen

Mary loves to make this smoothie with white peaches when they are available. During the summer, she shops the farmers' markets to find the sweetest peaches. It is a peach-tasting sensation with a subtle hint of raspberry.

1 CUP LOW-FAT PEACH YOGURT

¾ CUP PEACH NECTAR

½ CUP FRESH RASPBERRIES, FROZEN (SEE PAGE 22)

1½ CUPS DICED FRESH PEACHES, FROZEN (SEE PAGE 21)

Combine the yogurt and nectar in a blender. Add the raspberries and peaches. Blend until smooth.

SERVES 2

Apricots, cherries, nectarines, peaches, and plums are members of the stonefruit genus. Unlike other stonefruit, plums grow in clusters on the tree.

The name says it all. For a great start to your day, pour this smoothie over sliced bananas and top with Grape Nuts or wheat germ. The tangy taste of the buttermilk and plums will wake you up.

1 CUP LOW-FAT VANILLA YOGURT

$^1/_3$ CUP BUTTERMILK

$^1/_2$ CUP DICED STEWED PRUNES (RECIPE FOLLOWS)

$^1/_2$ CUP DICED FRESH PLUMS, FROZEN (SEE PAGE 21)

6 TO 8 ICE CUBES

Combine the yogurt and buttermilk in a blender. Add the prunes and plums. Blend until smooth. With the blender running, add the ice cubes one at a time until they are incorporated and the desired consistency is reached.

SERVES 2

plum

regular

STEWED PRUNES: Combine 2 cups pitted prunes and 1$^1/_2$ cups water in a medium saucepan; bring to a boil. Reduce heat and simmer for 15 minutes, or until soft. Let cool before using. Cover and refrigerate unused portion. Makes approximately 2 cups.

Make frozen pops by pouring your favorite smoothie into plastic frozen pop containers and freezing.

abc
easy as 1-2-3

Banana and coconut is a divine combination, and the addition of apricots makes this smoothie irresistible. The riper the apricots, the sweeter it will be. If you crave a smoothie with a little bite, use slightly tart apricots.

¾ CUP APRICOT NECTAR

½ CUP LIGHT COCONUT MILK

2 CUPS DICED FRESH APRICOTS, FROZEN (SEE PAGE 15)

1 FRESH BANANA, FROZEN AND SLICED (SEE PAGE 15)

Combine the nectar and coconut milk in a blender. Add the apricots and banana. Blend until smooth.

SERVES 2

bad boys

This stimulating blend of boysenberries and blueberries is a salute to the baddest of all boys. Its rich, creamy magenta appearance reflects its intense berry flavor.

1 1/2 CUPS LOW-FAT BOYSENBERRY YOGURT

3/4 CUP PASSION FRUIT SORBET

1 CUP FRESH BOYSENBERRIES, FROZEN (SEE PAGE 16)

1 CUP FRESH BLUEBERRIES, FROZEN (SEE PAGE 16)

Combine the yogurt and sorbet in a blender. Add the boysenberries and blueberries. Blend until smooth and strain through a sieve.

SERVES 2

The boysenberry is a hybrid of blackberries, raspberries, and loganberries.

nectarine
nelly

Toothsome and succulent nectarines are well matched with oranges and mango in this smoothie, which bursts with flavor. A glass of this brilliant orange concoction will add a little sunshine to your day.

1¼ CUPS ORANGE JUICE

2 CUPS DICED FRESH NECTARINES, FROZEN (SEE PAGE 19)

1 CUP DICED FRESH MANGO, FROZEN (SEE PAGE 19)

Pour the juice into a blender. Add the nectarines and mango. Blend until smooth.

SERVES 2

get yourself
a date!

This drink is an energy-giving source of carbohydrates, fiber, iron, and potassium—but be forewarned, it is not for calorie counters. If you can't get fresh dates, rehydrate dried ones simply by soaking them in hot water until soft.

$3/4$ CUP NONFAT PLAIN YOGURT

$1/2$ CUP NONFAT MILK

$1/4$ CUP DATES, PITTED AND CHOPPED (SEE PAGE 17)

2 FRESH BANANAS, FROZEN AND SLICED (SEE PAGE 15)

3 TABLESPOONS TAHINI

6 TO 8 ICE CUBES

Combine the yogurt and milk in a blender. Add the dates, bananas, and tahini. Blend until smooth. With the blender running, add the ice cubes one at a time until they are incorporated and the desired consistency is reached.

SERVES 2

Originally used for medicinal purposes, rhubarb once commanded more money than opium.

Rhubarb-strawberry pie is an American classic. This is like the pie without the crust! Drink this smoothie for a sweet treat after dinner.

- ½ CUP STRAWBERRY SORBET
- ½ CUP LOW-FAT STRAWBERRY YOGURT
- 1½ CUPS HULLED AND QUARTERED FRESH STRAWBERRIES, FROZEN (SEE PAGE 22)
- 1 CUP STEWED RHUBARB (RECIPE FOLLOWS)
- 1 FRESH BANANA, FROZEN AND SLICED (SEE PAGE 15)

Combine the sorbet and yogurt in a blender. Add the strawberries, rhubarb, and banana. Blend until smooth.

SERVES 2

STEWED RHUBARB: Combine 2 cups diced rhubarb and ½ cup apple juice in a medium saucepan; bring to a boil. Reduce heat and simmer for 12 to 15 minutes, or until soft. Let cool before using. Cover and refrigerate unused portion. Makes approximately 1 cup.

rhu-berry

43

mango
madness

Pour this smoothie into parfait glasses, add decorative straws, and serve as a dessert to your dinner guests. We offer a plate of ginger snaps for everyone to share.

$3/4$ CUP BUTTERMILK

$1/2$ CUP LOW-FAT VANILLA YOGURT

$2 1/2$ CUPS DICED FRESH MANGO, FROZEN (SEE PAGE 19)

1 TABLESPOON FRESH LIME JUICE (SEE PAGE 19)

1 TEASPOON GRATED AND CHOPPED FRESH GINGER

$1/4$ TEASPOON GROUND GINGER

3 TO 5 ICE CUBES

Combine the buttermilk and yogurt in a blender. Add the mango, lime juice, fresh ginger, and ground ginger. With the blender running, add the ice cubes one at a time until they are incorporated and the desired consistency is reached.

SERVES 2

44

maple blue

If you love blueberry cobbler, this smoothie is for you. It is a delightful combination of blueberries, maple, and cinnamon. Drink it for breakfast with pancakes or waffles.

1 CUP LOW-FAT BLUEBERRY YOGURT

3/4 CUP LOW-FAT MILK

1 TABLESPOON MAPLE SYRUP

1/2 TEASPOON GROUND CINNAMON

2 CUPS FRESH BLUEBERRIES, FROZEN (SEE PAGE 16)

Combine the yogurt, milk, syrup, and cinnamon in a blender. Add the blueberries and blend until smooth.

SERVES 2

starburst

Some say kiwi has a hint of strawberry flavor. This smoothie captures that elusive essence and explodes with taste. For the best results, make it in a food processor to avoid crushing the kiwi seeds, which causes them to be bitter.

3/4 CUP APPLE JUICE

1 CUP DICED FRESH KIWI (SEE PAGE 18)

1 CUP HULLED AND QUARTERED FRESH STRAWBERRIES, FROZEN (SEE PAGE 22)

2 FRESH BANANAS, FROZEN AND SLICED (SEE PAGE 15)

Place all the ingredients in a food processor. Process until smooth.

SERVES 2

black
beauty

Whether you pick your berries from the bramble or buy them in a basket, this smoothie is the perfect way to enjoy their fresh taste. Its creamy texture and very berry taste are a welcome treat anytime.

1 CUP LOW-FAT VANILLA YOGURT

½ CUP GRAPE JUICE

1½ CUPS FRESH BLUEBERRIES, FROZEN (SEE PAGE 16)

1 CUP FRESH BLACKBERRIES, FROZEN (SEE PAGE 15)

Combine the yogurt and grape juice in a blender. Add the berries. Blend until smooth and strain through a sieve.

SERVES 2

just
dew it!

This refreshing combination of honeydew melon and mint is a real thirst-quencher, ideal after a workout or on a hot summer day. It is extremely low in calories and fat but high in flavor.

2 $\frac{1}{2}$ CUPS DICED FRESH HONEYDEW MELON

2 TABLESPOONS CHOPPED FRESH MINT

1 TABLESPOON FRESH LIME JUICE

PINCH OF SALT

$\frac{1}{3}$ CUP GINGER ALE OR LEMON-LIME SODA

6 ICE CUBES

Place all the ingredients in a blender. Blend until smooth.

SERVES 2

Pack smoothies into self-sealing bags and freeze for to-go smoothies.

Dairy-lover or not, you will be wowed by these dynamic

nondairy combinations of fruit with sorbet, soy milk, tofu,

or rice milk. From ALMOND JOYOUS, with its choco-

late-almond flavor, to CRANZANIA'S puckery sweet-tart

taste, these smoothies will surprise, delight, and hook you.

no-moo blends

These are not just for vegans. These are for you, your

friends, your parents, and your boss. Make a few batches

of BIG BOLD BANANA, freeze them overnight, and

surprise the folks at work with breakfast. Or, the next

time your neighbor trims your hedges while doing their

own, pass them a glass of WATERMELON WAVELENGTH

and you'll never have to do your own yard work again.

tea-licious

This refreshing combination of peppermint and citrus is the perfect low-calorie and low-fat pick-me-up after working in the garden or playing a round of golf.

1 CUP STRONG-BREWED PEPPERMINT TEA, ROOM TEMPERATURE OR
   CHILLED
$\frac{1}{2}$ CUP LEMON SORBET
1$\frac{1}{2}$ CUPS FRESH ORANGE SEGMENTS, FROZEN (SEE PAGE 20)
$\frac{1}{2}$ CUP FRESH GRAPEFRUIT SEGMENTS, FROZEN (SEE PAGE 18)

Combine the tea and sorbet in a blender. Add the orange and grapefruit segments. Blend until smooth.

SERVES 2

Grapefruits were named for the way they grow in clusters—like grapes.

banana latte

This scrumptious drink looks and tastes like a real latte. With a coffee flavor and just a hint of banana, it's perfect for sipping over the Sunday paper.

1 CUP SOY MILK

$^3/_4$ CUP STRONG-BREWED COFFEE OR ESPRESSO, ROOM TEMPERATURE OR CHILLED

2 FRESH BANANAS, FROZEN AND SLICED (SEE PAGE 15)

6 TO 8 ICE CUBES

1 TEASPOON UNSWEETENED COCOA POWDER FOR GARNISH

$^1/_4$ TEASPOON GROUND CINNAMON FOR GARNISH

Combine the soy milk and coffee in a blender. Add the bananas. Blend until smooth. With the blender running, add ice cubes until they are incorporated and the desired consistency is reached. Pour into tall glasses and sprinkle with cocoa powder and cinnamon.

SERVES 2

watermelon wavelength

The inspiration for this refreshing combination came from our friend Marcela, who loves to mix lemonade with watermelon juice. It is a light and delicious smoothie that is low in calories and fat.

$1^1/_2$ CUPS DICED SEEDED WATERMELON

$^3/_4$ CUP LEMON SORBET

8 ICE CUBES

1 TABLESPOON FRESH LEMON JUICE

PINCH OF SALT

Place all the ingredients in a blender. Blend until smooth.

SERVES 2

54

sweet
cherry-ot

Sara and Mary go mad for the taste of cherry pie, which they grew up eating every summer back in North Carolina. Now, when they hunger for a taste of home, they make this very cherry smoothie to satisfy their craving.

- 1 1/4 CUPS UNSWEETENED CHERRY JUICE
- 1/4 CUP RASPBERRY SORBET
- 1 1/2 CUPS HALVED AND PITTED FRESH CHERRIES, FROZEN (SEE PAGE 16)
- 1 CUP PEELED AND DICED FRESH PEACHES, FROZEN (SEE PAGE 21)

Combine the cherry juice and sorbet in a blender. Add the cherries and peaches. Blend until smooth.

SERVES 2

big bold
banana

Some like it big, some like it bold. Whichever way you prefer it, this is the
smoothie for you. Packed with potassium and protein, it's great before
exercising, or you can freeze it and take it along on a hike. It will thaw
and be ready to drink when you've reached your peak.

$3/4$ CUP SOY MILK

$1/2$ CUP SOFT SILKEN TOFU

4 FRESH BANANAS, FROZEN AND SLICED (SEE PAGE 15)

1 TABLESPOON HONEY

1 TABLESPOON VANILLA EXTRACT

1 TABLESPOON CAROB POWDER

Combine the soy milk and tofu in a blender. Add the bananas, honey,
vanilla extract, and carob powder. Blend until smooth.

SERVES 2

cran-
zania

Cranberries aren't just for Thanksgiving anymore—this sweet-tart smoothie proves that. This union of cranberries and oranges is ideal for winter, when both fruits are at the peak of their season. Its high vitamin C content will help chase away colds.

1 ¼ CUPS CRANBERRY JUICE

½ CUP RASPBERRY SORBET

1 TABLESPOON ORANGE JUICE CONCENTRATE

1 ½ CUPS FRESH ORANGE SEGMENTS, FROZEN (SEE PAGE 20)

½ CUP FRESH CRANBERRIES, FROZEN (SEE PAGE 17)

Combine the cranberry juice, sorbet, and orange juice concentrate in a blender. Add the orange segments and cranberries. Blend until smooth.

SERVES 2

Also called bounce berries, cranberries hail from the Northeast, where they fare well in lowland bogs.

peanut
power

This blend of chocolate, bananas, and peanuts is for the junior varsity member trying to make varsity or for the wimp tired of having sand kicked in his face by bullies. In preparation for a long day, we whip up this smoothie and serve it with a whole-wheat bagel for a high-energy, high-fiber breakfast.

$\frac{1}{2}$ CUP CHOCOLATE RICE MILK

$\frac{1}{2}$ CUP SOFT SILKEN TOFU

$\frac{1}{3}$ CUP CREAMY PEANUT BUTTER

2 FRESH BANANAS, FROZEN AND SLICED (SEE PAGE 15)

2 TABLESPOONS CHOCOLATE SYRUP

6 ICE CUBES

Combine the rice milk, tofu, and peanut butter in a blender. Add the bananas, chocolate syrup, and ice cubes. Blend until smooth.

SERVES 2

The delectable, sensual peach was once used as a love token in China.

pea-pine-fu

For those of you who turn up your noses at tofu, this golden smoothie will fool your taste buds. The dynamic combination of peach and pineapple are the prominent flavors, while the tofu adds the creamy texture.

$^3/_4$ CUP PEACH SORBET

$^3/_4$ CUP WHITE GRAPE JUICE

$^1/_2$ CUP SOFT SILKEN TOFU

1 TABLESPOON FRESH LIME JUICE

$1^1/_2$ CUPS PEELED AND DICED FRESH PEACHES, FROZEN (SEE PAGE 21)

1 CUP DICED FRESH PINEAPPLE, FROZEN (SEE PAGE 21)

Combine the sorbet, grape juice, tofu, and lime juice in a blender. Add the peaches and pineapple. Blend until smooth.

SERVES 2

california ambrosia

You don't have to wear Birkenstocks to enjoy this smoothie. Pairing mango with mint results in a fabulous flavor combination that true Californians will serve with a side of alfalfa sprouts.

1 CUP MANGO NECTAR

½ CUP SOFT SILKEN TOFU

2 TEASPOONS FRESH LIME JUICE

1½ CUPS DICED FRESH MANGO, FROZEN (SEE PAGE 19)

2 TABLESPOONS CHOPPED FRESH MINT

3 TO 5 ICE CUBES

Combine the nectar, tofu, and lime juice in a blender. Add the mango and mint. With the blender running, add the ice cubes one at a time until they are incorporated and the desired consistency is reached.

SERVES 2

almond joyous

This is a delicious rendition of the infamous Almond Joy candy bar. Its luscious balance of chocolate, coconut, and almonds will make you feel like a nut.

1 CUP LIGHT COCONUT MILK

1½ CUPS CHOCOLATE SORBET

2 FRESH BANANAS, FROZEN AND SLICED (SEE PAGE 15)

2 TABLESPOONS GRATED COCONUT (OPTIONAL)

1 TEASPOON COCONUT EXTRACT

¾ TEASPOON ALMOND EXTRACT

Combine the coconut milk and sorbet in a blender. Add the bananas, coconut (if using), coconut extract, and almond extract. Blend until smooth.

SERVES 2

polynesian
power
punch

We served this taste-of-the-tropics smoothie at a Caribbean-theme brunch. Its fresh fruit taste, along with paper parasols and colorful straws, really enhanced our festive morning.

- ½ CUP LIGHT COCONUT MILK
- ½ CUP GUAVA NECTAR
- ½ CUP STRAWBERRY SORBET
- 1½ CUPS HULLED AND QUARTERED FRESH STRAWBERRIES, FROZEN (SEE PAGE 22)
- 1 CUP DICED FRESH PINEAPPLE, FROZEN (SEE PAGE 21)

Combine the coconut milk, guava nectar, and sorbet in a blender. Add the strawberries and pineapple. Blend until smooth.

SERVES 2

Use a sports bottle with a straw attached as a reusable smoothie container.

eastern

enlightenment

Chai is a distinctive blend of Indian black teas flavored with aromatic and flavorful spices—clove, ginger, and cardamom. It is available from specialty shops, coffee retailers, and natural foods stores. Here it is complemented by peaches and papaya. Try this smoothie instead of coffee in the morning.

1 $\frac{1}{4}$ CUPS STRONG-BREWED CHAI, ROOM TEMPERATURE OR CHILLED

$\frac{3}{4}$ CUP PEACH SORBET

1 CUP PEELED AND DICED FRESH PEACHES, FROZEN (SEE PAGE 21)

$\frac{3}{4}$ CUP DICED FRESH PAPAYA, FROZEN (SEE PAGE 20)

1 TABLESPOON FRESH LEMON JUICE

Combine the chai and sorbet in a blender. Add peaches, papaya, and lemon juice. Blend until smooth.

SERVES 2

pink lady

This smoothie reminds us of our favorite candy, Jolly Rancher watermelon sticks. Mary and Sara made this for a friend's baby shower and served it with little pink ribbons tied around the stems of the glasses.

1 ½ CUPS DICED WATERMELON

½ CUP STRAWBERRY SORBET

8 ICE CUBES

1 TABLESPOON FRESH LEMON JUICE

PINCH OF SALT

Place all the ingredients in a blender. Blend until smooth.

SERVES 2

Watermelons are 90 percent water.

These rich and creamy combinations of fruit and frozen

yogurt are not for the weakhearted. Because they are so

outrageously delicious, it will take every ounce of will-

power you have to prevent you from eating both servings.

Scrumptious PLANET PINEAPPLE will direct you to a new

universe, lavish RAZZY STAR will make you sing, and lush

SMOOTHIE À LA KING will start your pelvis rockin'.

decadent medleys

Sneak a RASPBERRY CAPPUCCINO in during the after-

noon, plant yourself in front of the television with an

UNCANNY CANTALOUPE, or treat everyone around the

dinner table to APPLE À LA MODE once the dirty dishes

have been cleared.

cool hand lime

One of our favorite movies, *Cool Hand Luke*, was the inspiration for this delectably creamy lime dessert. For special-occasion dinners, serve it between courses as a palate cleanser.

¾ CUP LOW-FAT MILK

½ CUP FRESH LIME SEGMENTS, FROZEN (SEE PAGE 19)

3 TABLESPOONS FRESH LIME JUICE

3 CUPS NONFAT VANILLA FROZEN YOGURT

Place all the ingredients in a blender. Blend until smooth.

SERVES 2

Limes have played an important role in history—British soldiers once ate them to prevent scurvy.

cheesecake

Serve this luscious strawberry dessert smoothie with a plate of graham crackers, and you'll never want to eat cheesecake the traditional way again.

1¼ CUP NONFAT STRAWBERRY FROZEN YOGURT

¾ CUP STRAWBERRY NECTAR

¼ CUP LOW-FAT SOUR CREAM

3 TABLESPOONS CREAM CHEESE

2 CUPS HULLED AND QUARTERED FRESH STRAWBERRIES, FROZEN
(SEE PAGE 22)

Combine the frozen yogurt, nectar, sour cream, and cream cheese in a blender. Add the strawberries and blend until smooth.

SERVES 2

Pineapples have long been symbols of hospitality. Serve this creamy pineapple smoothie to your guests and they may just linger in hopes of seconds.

1 CUP LIGHT COCONUT MILK

2 CUPS NONFAT VANILLA FROZEN YOGURT

1 CUP DICED FRESH PINEAPPLE, FROZEN (SEE PAGE 21)

1 TABLESPOON FRESH LEMON JUICE (SEE PAGE 19)

Place ingredients in a blender. Blend until smooth.

SERVES 2

planet pineapple

75

apple
à la mode

Make this smoothie for the apple of your eye, because not only is it rich and delicious, apples contain pectin, a fiber that helps to reduce cholesterol.

2 CUPS NONFAT VANILLA FROZEN YOGURT

¾ CUP UNSWEETENED APPLESAUCE (RECIPE FOLLOWS)

¼ CUP CHILLED APPLE JUICE

1 CUP DICED FRESH APPLE, FROZEN (SEE PAGE 15)

½ TEASPOON GROUND CINNAMON

¼ TEASPOON GROUND NUTMEG

Combine the frozen yogurt, applesauce, and apple juice in a blender. Add the apple, cinnamon, and nutmeg. Blend until smooth.

SERVES 2

APPLESAUCE: Combine 1 cup chopped peeled apple and 1 cup water in a small saucepan; bring to a boil. Reduce heat and simmer for about 10 minutes, or until the apples are tender and the water is evaporated. Mash with a fork. Let cool before using. Cover and refrigerate unused portion. Makes about 1 cup.

cherry pop

Yowza, this one is good! Sweet and sticky, this smoothie is right on the money for replicating a cherry coke.

3/4 CUPS COLA

2 CUPS PITTED AND HALVED FRESH CHERRIES, FROZEN
   (SEE PAGE 16)

1 CUP NONFAT VANILLA FROZEN YOGURT

1 TEASPOON FRESH LEMON JUICE (SEE PAGE 19)

1 TEASPOON CHERRY EXTRACT (OPTIONAL)

Place all the ingredients in a blender. Blend until smooth.

SERVES 2

smoothie à la king

Long live the King! This rich and oh-so-fattening combination of peanut butter and bananas was one of Elvis's favorites. If he were alive today, this would be the smoothie he would drink—and he'd be thrilled to know it's a great source of potassium and calcium.

- ¾ CUP NONFAT MILK
- ¾ CUP NONFAT VANILLA FROZEN YOGURT
- ⅓ CUP CREAMY PEANUT BUTTER
- 2 FRESH BANANAS, FROZEN AND SLICED (SEE PAGE 15)

Place all the ingredients in a blender. Blend until smooth.

SERVES 2

razzy star

This decadent smoothie is named for one of Sara's favorite bands, Mazzy Star, and was inspired by her favorite combination—raspberries and cream. For parties, Mary and Sara enhance this dessert by substituting heavy cream for the milk, layering the smoothie with fresh raspberries in parfait glasses, and topping it with whipped cream.

- ¾ CUP LOW-FAT PLAIN YOGURT
- ½ CUP LOW-FAT MILK
- 1 CUP FRESH RASPBERRIES, FROZEN (SEE PAGE 22)
- 1 CUP RASPBERRY SORBET

Place all the ingredients in a blender. Blend until smooth.

SERVES 2

Mary and Sara like to serve this orange and chocolate taste sensation in hollowed-out oranges. After they make the smoothie, they refreeze it, and then scoop it into oranges and garnish with chocolate straws.

1 1/2 CUPS NONFAT VANILLA FROZEN YOGURT

1/2 CUP ORANGE JUICE

1/4 CUP KAHLÙA

1 1/2 CUPS FRESH ORANGE SEGMENTS, FROZEN (SEE PAGE 20)

1/4 CUP CHOCOLATE CHIPS

2 TABLESPOONS FROZEN ORANGE CONCENTRATE

3 TO 5 ICE CUBES

Place the frozen yogurt, orange juice, and Kahlùa in a blender. Add the orange segments, chocolate chips, and orange concentrate. Blend until smooth. With the blender running, add the ice cubes one at a time until they are incorporated and the desired consistency is reached.

SERVES 2

mocha
à l'orange

jitterbug

This combination of coffee and hazelnut will make you a "jitterbug." For a change of pace, substitute vanilla, almond, or your favorite flavor syrup for the hazelnut syrup. Flavored syrups are usually available in the coffee aisle of supermarkets or at coffee bars.

1 CUP STRONG-BREWED COFFEE, ROOM TEMPERATURE OR CHILLED
2 CUPS NONFAT VANILLA FROZEN YOGURT
2 FRESH BANANAS, FROZEN AND SLICED (SEE PAGE 15)
1 TABLESPOON HAZELNUT-FLAVORED SYRUP

Place all the ingredients in a blender. Blend until smooth.

SERVES 2

kiwi kiss

If you aren't a kiwi lover now, you will be after your first taste. For the best results, make this bright green smoothie in a food processor to avoid crushing the kiwi seeds, which causes them to be bitter. The sparkling taste of kiwi shines in each sip.

1¾ CUPS DICED FRESH KIWI (SEE PAGE 18)
1½ CUPS LIME SHERBET
1 CUP DICED FRESH HONEYDEW MELON (SEE PAGE 18)

Place all the ingredients in a food processor. Process until smooth.

SERVES 2

sassy frass

Reminiscent of root beer floats served at an old-fashioned soda fountain, this smoothie is full of flavor. Drink it as is, or pour into a frosted glass of root beer for a true float.

1 CUP ROOT BEER
1 CUP NONFAT VANILLA FROZEN YOGURT
2 FRESH BANANAS, FROZEN AND SLICED (SEE PAGE 15)
½ TEASPOON FRESH LEMON JUICE

Place all the ingredients in a blender. Blend until smooth.

SERVES 2

This ultra-refreshing combination of summer fruits makes a complete lunch alongside a bowl of cottage cheese.

2 CUPS DICED CANTALOUPE

2 CUPS DICED FRESH PLUMS, FROZEN (SEE PAGE 21)

1 CUP ORANGE SHERBET

1 TABLESPOON FRESH LEMON JUICE (OPTIONAL)

PINCH OF SALT

Place all the ingredients in a blender. Blend until smooth.

SERVES 2

The melon commonly known as a cantaloupe is actually a muskmelon; true cantaloupe is rarely found outside Europe.

raspberry
cappuccino

On a hot summer day there isn't anything as refreshing and motivating as this lavish espresso smoothie. The rich taste of chocolate and coffee is well matched by the berries.

$^3/_4$ CUP LOW-FAT CHOCOLATE MILK

$^1/_3$ CUP ESPRESSO OR 1 TABLESPOON INSTANT COFFEE DISSOLVED IN $^1/_3$ CUP WATER, ROOM TEMPERATURE OR CHILLED

2 TABLESPOONS CHOCOLATE SYRUP

$1^1/_2$ CUPS NONFAT COFFEE FROZEN YOGURT

1 CUP FRESH RASPBERRIES, FROZEN (SEE PAGE 22)

$^1/_2$ CUP COLD NONFAT MILK

UNSWEETENED CHOCOLATE POWDER FOR GARNISH

Combine the chocolate milk, espresso, and chocolate syrup in a blender. Add the frozen yogurt and raspberries. Blend until smooth. Pour into 2 glasses. Rinse out the blender container. Pour the milk into the blender and blend on high speed until frothy, about 15 seconds. Divide between the smoothies and sprinkle them with chocolate powder.

SERVES 2

These smoothies were invented for a relaxing after-

noon on the deck, a party on the patio, or a romantic

evening in front of the fireplace. They are at once as old

as the moon and as new as your next blink—the classic

screwdriver becomes a BLOODY ORANGE, a mimosa

turns into NECTAR OF THE GODS, and a margarita

is transformed into a blissful SUNSET SIPPER.

drunken
concoctions

Blend a batch of GIN SIN after a day of spring ski-

ing. Or, surprise holiday dinner guests with GOLDEN

GIRL as an aperitif. These delectable combinations go

down easy, but sip them slowly to savor every drop.

tropical teaser

Can't take off for the islands? This tropical fruit blend with a touch of rum is the next best thing. It will transport you in mind and spirit to a warm balmy evening on a white sandy beach.

$1/2$ CUP LIGHT COCONUT MILK

$1/2$ CUP RUM

1 CUP DICED FRESH PINEAPPLE, FROZEN (SEE PAGE 21)

1 CUP DICED FRESH MANGO, FROZEN (SEE PAGE 19)

1 FRESH BANANA, FROZEN AND SLICED (SEE PAGE 15)

Combine the coconut milk and rum in a blender. Add pineapple, mango, and banana. Blend until smooth.

SERVES 2

In India, where mangoes originate, the mango tree is considered sacred.

nectar of the gods

When Sara was planning Mary's wedding shower, she created this drink as an alternative to mimosas. The result is a sparkling blend of peaches and champagne fit for the gods.

1 CUP ORANGE JUICE

1 CUP PEACH SORBET

3 TABLESPOONS BRANDY

2 CUPS PEELED AND DICED FRESH PEACHES, FROZEN (SEE PAGE 21)

1 CUP CHAMPAGNE

Place all the ingredients in a blender. Blend until smooth.

SERVES 2

savvy sangria

This is the cocktail to serve poolside. Make it a party by serving tapas with this robust smoothie. The taste of citrus, plums, and grapes complements the red wine.

¾ CUPS CHILLED LIGHT FRUITY RED WINE, SUCH AS A PINOT NOIR

⅓ CUP RED GRAPE JUICE

½ CUP LEMON SORBET

2 TABLESPOONS ORANGE CONCENTRATE

½ CUP FRESH GRAPES, FROZEN (SEE PAGE 17)

1 CUP DICED FRESH PLUMS, FROZEN (SEE PAGE 21)

Place all the ingredients in a blender. Blend until smooth.

SERVES 2

This twist on the traditional screwdriver is sublime. When blood oranges are at their sweetest, from December to February, use them in place of regular oranges.

3 1/2 CUPS FRESH ORANGE SEGMENTS, FROZEN (SEE PAGE 20)
3/4 CUP VODKA
1 TABLESPOON ORANGE CONCENTRATE
1 TABLESPOON GRAND MARNIER

Place all the ingredients in a blender. Blend until smooth.

SERVES 2

bloody orange

Because grapefruits are sweetest during the winter, make this drink as a delightful and surprising holiday aperitif. It's also a great way to beat a sore throat during cold season—the cloves have a numbing effect and it's packed with vitamin C.

1/2 CUP GIN
1 TABLESPOON PLUS 1 TEASPOON ORANGE-FLAVORED LIQUEUR
3 CUPS FRESH GRAPEFRUIT SEGMENTS, PREFERABLY PINK, FROZEN (SEE PAGE 18)
1/8 TEASPOON GROUND CLOVES
8 ICE CUBES

Combine all the ingredients in a blender. Blend until smooth.

SERVES 2

gin sin

golden girl

Sauternes is an intensely sweet and complex dessert wine from a region of the same name in France. We've created a dynamite combination of pears and Sauternes that is perfect for serving as an after-dinner drink in decorative frosted glasses. For a nonalcoholic version, substitute pear nectar for the Sauternes.

¾ CUP SAUTERNES OR OTHER SWEET DESSERT WINE

1¾ CUPS DICED FRESH PEARS, FROZEN (SEE PAGE 21)

½ CUP DICED FRESH APRICOTS, FROZEN (SEE PAGE 15)

1 TEASPOON FRESH LEMON JUICE

Place all the ingredients in a blender. Blend until smooth.

SERVES 2

sunset sipper

Once you try this concoction of sweet pineapple and tequila you will never want a regular margarita again. Serve in salt-rimmed margarita glasses, accompanied by tortilla chips and a fruit salsa.

$^1/_4$ CUP TEQUILA

3 TABLESPOONS TRIPLE SEC

3 TABLESPOONS COINTREAU

3 TABLESPOONS FRESH LIME JUICE

$^1/_4$ CUP PINEAPPLE JUICE

3 CUPS DICED FRESH PINEAPPLE, FROZEN (SEE PAGE 21)

Place all the ingredients in a blender. Blend until smooth.

SERVES 2

The English named the pineapple for its close resemblance to the pinecone.

nutritional analyses

ABC, EASY AS 1-2-3

Per 12-fluid-ounce serving: calories 191; total fat 3.8 g; cholesterol 0 g; carbohydrates 38.6 g; dietary fiber 4.9 g; protein 2.7 g; sodium 27 mg; potassium 677 mg; calcium 29 mg; iron 1.3 mg; vitamin A 5000 i.u.; vitamin C 18 mg.

ALMOND JOYOUS

Per 12-fluid-ounce serving (including optional coconut): calories 264; total fat 8.4 g; cholesterol 0 g; carbohydrates 44.6 g; dietary fiber 2.4 g; protein 0.9 g; sodium 64 mg; potassium 313 mg; calcium 5 mg; iron 0.3 mg; vitamin A 60 i.u.; vitamin C 7 mg.

APPLE À LA MODE

Per 12-fluid-ounce serving: calories 281; total fat 0.4 g; cholesterol 0 g; carbohydrates 58.9 g; dietary fiber 2.9 g; protein 7.3 g; sodium 4 mg; potassium 204 mg; calcium 121 mg; iron 0.9 mg; vitamin A 209 i.u.; vitamin C 6 mg.

BAD BOYS

Per 12-fluid-ounce serving: calories 287; total fat 2.4 g; cholesterol 8 g; carbohydrates 61.4 g; dietary fiber 4.7 g; protein 8 g; sodium 97 mg; potassium 456 mg; calcium 258 mg; iron 0.8 mg; vitamin A 199 i.u.; vitamin C 12 mg.

BANANA LATTE

Per 12-fluid-ounce serving: calories 112; total fat 2.8 g; cholesterol 0 g; carbohydrates 20.6 g; dietary fiber 3.8 g; protein 4.3 g; sodium 17 mg; potassium 526 mg; calcium 16 mg; iron 1.2 mg; vitamin A 99 i.u.; vitamin C 7 mg.

BIG BOLD BANANA

Per 12-fluid-ounce serving: calories 255; total fat 4.8 g; cholesterol 0 g; carbohydrates 49.6 g; dietary fiber 6.6 g; protein 8.2 g; sodium 17 mg; potassium 806 mg; calcium 76 mg; iron 3.8 mg; vitamin A 192 i.u.; vitamin C 14 mg.

BLACK BEAUTY
Per 12-fluid-ounce serving: calories 231; total fat 2.1 g; cholesterol 6 g; carbohydrates 49 g; dietary fiber 6.4 g; protein 7.2 g; sodium 83 mg; potassium 563 mg; calcium 229 mg; iron 0.8 mg; vitamin A 287 i.u.; vitamin C 29 mg.

BLOODY ORANGE
Per 12-fluid-ounce serving: calories 341; total fat 0.3 g; cholesterol 0 g; carbohydrates 32.8 g; dietary fiber 5.6 g; protein 2.4 g; sodium 1 mg; potassium 477 mg; calcium 95 mg; iron 0.3 mg; vitamin A 496 i.u.; vitamin C 135 mg.

CALIFORNIA AMBROSIA
Per 12-fluid-ounce serving: calories 172; total fat 3 g; cholesterol 0 g; carbohydrates 34.8 g; dietary fiber 2.9 g; protein 5.3 g; sodium 15 mg; potassium 277 mg; calcium 105 mg; iron 4.7 mg; vitamin A 3519 i.u.; vitamin C 34 mg.

CHERRY POP
Per 12-fluid-ounce serving: calories 200; total fat 0.7 g; cholesterol 0 g; carbohydrates 43.4 g; dietary fiber 1.5 g; protein 4.9 g; sodium 5 mg; potassium 196 mg; calcium 75 mg; iron 1 mg; vitamin A 1426 i.u.; vitamin C 4 mg.

COOKIES AND CREAM
Per 12-fluid-ounce serving: calories 443; total fat 8.9 g; cholesterol 4 g; carbohydrates 79.9 g; dietary fiber 1.8 g; protein 13.4 g; sodium 277 mg; potassium 828 mg; calcium 393 mg; iron 1.3 mg; vitamin A 196 i.u.; vitamin C 9 mg.

COOL HAND LIME
Per 12-fluid-ounce serving: calories 337; total fat 1.9 g; cholesterol 7 g; carbohydrates 61.2 g; dietary fiber 1.5 g; protein 14.0 g; sodium 47 mg; potassium 217 mg; calcium 284 mg; iron 0.6 mg; vitamin A 424 i.u.; vitamin C 24 mg.

CRANZANIA
Per 12-fluid-ounce serving: calories 162; total fat 0.3 g; cholesterol 0 g; carbohydrates 48.8 g; dietary fiber 3.4 g; protein 1.2 g; sodium 7 mg; potassium 283 mg; calcium 49 mg; iron 0.4 mg; vitamin A 243 i.u.; vitamin C 124 mg.

DANGEROUSLY RED
Per 12-fluid-ounce serving: calories 209; total fat 2.1 g; cholesterol 5 g; carbohydrates 44.5 g; dietary fiber 6.4g; protein 5.7 g; sodium 63 mg;

potassium 477 mg; calcium 187 mg; iron 0.9 mg; vitamin A 163 i.u.; vitamin C 97 mg.

EASTERN ENLIGHTENMENT
Per 12-fluid-ounce serving: calories 151; total fat 0.1 g; cholesterol 0 g; carbohydrates 37.2 g; dietary fiber 3.5 g; protein 3.2 g; sodium 30 mg; potassium 1652 mg; calcium 25 mg; iron 1 mg; vitamin A 556 i.u.; vitamin C 31 mg.

GET YOURSELF A DATE!
Per 12-fluid-ounce serving: calories 282; total fat 12.8 g; cholesterol 3 g; carbohydrates 33.7 g; dietary fiber 3.2 g; protein 12.1 g; sodium 102 mg; potassium 758 mg; calcium 482 mg; iron 4.9 mg; vitamin A 203 i.u.; vitamin C 8 mg.

GIN SIN
Per 12-fluid-ounce serving: calories 292; total fat 0.4 g; cholesterol 0 g; carbohydrates 31.2 g; dietary fiber 3.8 g; protein 2.2 g; sodium 4 mg; potassium 481 mg; calcium 44 mg; iron 0.3 mg; vitamin A 429 i.u.; vitamin C 119 mg.

GOLDEN GIRL
Per 12-fluid-ounce serving: calories 219; total fat 0.3 g; cholesterol 0 g; carbohydrates 31.3 g; dietary fiber 3.8 g; protein 1.7 g; sodium 8 mg; potassium 485 mg; calcium 20 mg; iron 0.6 mg; vitamin A 1729 i.u.; vitamin C 15 mg.

GUAVA GULP
Per 12-fluid-ounce serving: calories 163; total fat 0.7 g; cholesterol 0 g; carbohydrates 42.7 g; dietary fiber 8.3 g; protein 1.5 g; sodium 9 mg; potassium 665 mg; calcium 25 mg; iron 0.5 mg; vitamin A 4901 i.u.; vitamin C 254 mg.

JITTERBUG
Per 12-fluid-ounce serving: calories 271; total fat .04 g; cholesterol 0 g; carbohydrates 56.4 g; dietary fiber 1.9 g; protein 8.1 g; sodium 12 mg; potassium 378 mg; calcium 111 mg; iron 0.7 mg; vitamin A 216 i.u.; vitamin C 8 mg.

JUST DEW IT!
Per 12-fluid-ounce serving: calories 51; total fat 0.1 g; cholesterol 0 g; carbo-hydrates 13.3 g; dietary fiber 0.6 g; protein 0.5 g; sodium 81 mg; potassium 277 mg; calcium 12 mg; iron 0.3 mg; vitamin A 40 i.u.; vitamin C 27 mg.

KIWI KISS
Per 12-fluid-ounce serving: calories 324; total fat 3.7 g; cholesterol 11 g; carbohydrates 73.7 g; dietary fiber 6.4 g; protein 3.7 g; sodium 79 mg; potassium 865 mg; calcium 128 mg; iron 1 mg; vitamin A 1765 i.u.; vitamin C 195 mg.

MANGO MADNESS
Per 12-fluid-ounce serving: calories 182; total fat 1.9 g; cholesterol 6 g; carbohydrates 37.5 g; dietary fiber 2.6 g; protein 6.6 g; sodium 138 mg; potassium 502 mg; calcium 220 mg; iron 0.3 mg; vitamin A 5624 i.u.; vitamin C 43 mg.

MAPLE BLUE
Per 12-fluid-ounce serving: calories 265; total fat 3.6 g; cholesterol 12 g; carbohydrates 52.7 g; dietary fiber 4.1 g; protein 8.5 g; sodium 116 mg; potassium 492 mg; calcium 290 mg; iron 0.7 mg; vitamin A 387 i.u.; vitamin C 20 mg.

MOCHA À L'ORANGE
Per 12-fluid-ounce serving: calories 456; total fat 6.7 g; cholesterol 0 g; carbohydrates 79.3 g; dietary fiber 3.9 g; protein 8 g; sodium 7 mg; potassium 510 mg; calcium 137 mg; iron 1.1 mg; vitamin A 494 i.u.; vitamin C 109 mg.

NECTARINE NELLY
Per 12-fluid-ounce serving: calories 168; total fat 1 g; cholesterol 0 g; carbohydrates 40.4 g; dietary fiber 3.3 g; protein 2.5 g; sodium 3 mg; potassium 661 mg; calcium 29 mg; iron 0.6 mg; vitamin A 3446 i.u.; vitamin C 100 mg.

NECTAR OF THE GODS
Per 12-fluid-ounce serving: calories 400; total fat 0.4 g; cholesterol 0 g; carbohydrates 65.3 g; dietary fiber 6.6 g; protein 2.1 g; sodium 1 mg; potassium 583 mg; calcium 22 mg; iron 0.4 mg; vitamin A 1158 i.u.; vitamin C 79 mg.

PASSION!
Per 12-fluid-ounce serving: calories 231; total fat 3.3 g; cholesterol 11 g; carbohydrates 50 g; dietary fiber 1.9 g; protein 3.6 g; sodium 48 mg; potassium 435 mg; calcium 113 mg; iron 0.6 mg; vitamin A 574 i.u.; vitamin C 39 mg.

PEACHY KEEN
Per 12-fluid-ounce serving: calories 232; total fat 1.6 g; cholesterol 5 g;

carbohydrates 51.7 g; dietary fiber 4.6 g; protein 5.9 g; sodium 67 mg; potassium 534 mg; calcium 175 mg; iron 0.6 mg; vitamin A 1017 i.u.; vitamin C 41 mg.

PEANUT POWER

Per 12-fluid-ounce serving: calories 436; total fat 25.3 g; cholesterol 0 g; carbohydrates 46 g; dietary fiber 6.1 g; protein 16.5 g; sodium 253 mg; potassium 747 mg; calcium 84 mg; iron 4.4 mg; vitamin A 108 i.u.; vitamin C 7 mg.

PEA-PINE-FU

Per 12-fluid-ounce serving: calories 190; total fat 2.9 g; cholesterol 0 g; carbohydrates 51.9 g; dietary fiber 4.2 g; protein 5.8 g; sodium 13 mg; potassium 532 mg; calcium 73 mg; iron 3.3 mg; vitamin A 751 i.u.; vitamin C 23 mg.

PINK LADY

Per 12-fluid-ounce serving: calories 70; total fat 0.5 g; cholesterol 0 g; carbohydrates 17 g; dietary fiber 0.8 g; protein 0.8 g; sodium 73 mg; potassium 149 mg; calcium 12 mg; iron 0.2 mg; vitamin A 441 i.u.; vitamin C 15 mg.

PLANET PINEAPPLE

Per 12-fluid-ounce serving: calories 318; total fat 6.7 g; cholesterol 4 g; carbohydrates 50.9 g; dietary fiber 1.0 g; protein 11.9 g; sodium 200 mg; potassium 615 mg; calcium 410 mg; iron 0.5 mg; vitamin A 33 i.u.; vitamin C 17 mg.

PLUM REGULAR

Per 12-fluid-ounce serving: calories 484; total fat 2.8 g; cholesterol 7 g; carbohydrates 114.3 g; dietary fiber 11.0 g; protein 11.1 g; sodium 131 mg; potassium 1466 mg; calcium 323 mg; iron 3.8 mg; vitamin A 3104 i.u.; vitamin C 10 mg.

POLYNESIAN POWER PUNCH

Per 12-fluid-ounce serving: calories 141; total fat 3.8 g; cholesterol 0 g; carbohydrates 34.8 g; dietary fiber 3.7 g; protein 1.0 g; sodium 31 mg; potassium 281 mg; calcium 26 mg; iron 0.9 mg; vitamin A 116 i.u.; vitamin C 73 mg.

RASPBERRY CAPPUCCINO

Per 12-fluid-ounce serving: calories 292; total fat 2.5 g; cholesterol 8 g; carbohydrates 55.6 g; dietary fiber 4.6 g; protein 11.5 g; sodium 106 mg; potassium 400 mg; calcium 282 mg; iron 1.2 mg; vitamin A 512 i.u.; vitamin C 17 mg.

RAZZY STAR

Per 12-fluid-ounce serving: calories 233; total fat 2.8 g; cholesterol 10 g; carbohydrates 45.8 g; dietary fiber 7 g; protein 7 g; sodium 90 mg; potassium 383 mg; calcium 243 mg; iron 0.4 mg; vitamin A 258 i.u.; vitamin C 22 mg.

RHU-BERRY

Per 12-fluid-ounce serving: calories 200; total fat 1.5 g; cholesterol 3 g; carbohydrates 45.8 g; dietary fiber 5.1 g; protein 4.1 g; sodium 38 mg; potassium 759 mg; calcium 179 mg; iron 1 mg; vitamin A 178 i.u.; vitamin C 71 mg.

SASSY FRASS

Per 12-fluid-ounce serving: calories 209; total fat 0.4 g; cholesterol 0 g; carbohydrates 47 g; dietary fiber 1.8 g; protein 4.3 g; sodium 17 mg; potassium 296 mg; calcium 62 mg; iron 0.4 mg; vitamin A 137 i.u.; vitamin C 8 mg.

SAVVY SANGRIA

Per 12-fluid-ounce serving: calories 245; total fat 0.7 g; cholesterol 0 g; carbohydrates 47 g; dietary fiber 2.1 g; protein 1.7 g; sodium 10 mg; potassium 484 mg; calcium 25 mg; iron 0.7 mg; vitamin A 343 i.u.; vitamin C 35 mg.

SMOOTHIE À LA KING

Per 12-fluid-ounce serving: calories 430; total fat 22.2 g; cholesterol 3 g; carbohydrates 45.6 g; dietary fiber 4.3 g; protein 18.8 g; sodium 312 mg; potassium 950 mg; calcium 284 mg; iron 1.1 mg; vitamin A 253 i.u.; vitamin C 8 mg.

SMOOTHIE CLASSICO

Per 12-fluid-ounce serving: calories 145; total fat 0.9 g; cholesterol 0 g; carbohydrates 35.3 g; dietary fiber 3.6 g; protein 2.1 g; sodium 3 mg; potassium 658 mg; calcium 28 mg; iron 0.7 mg; vitamin A 327 i.u.; vitamin C 108 mg.

STARBURST

Per 12-fluid-ounce serving: calories 195; total fat 1.2 g; cholesterol 0 g; carbohydrates 48.3 g; dietary fiber 6.9 g; protein 2.2 g; sodium 9 mg; potassium 858 mg; calcium 47 mg; iron 1.3 mg; vitamin A 258 i.u.; vitamin C 147 mg.

STRAWBERRY CHEESECAKE
Per 12-fluid-ounce serving: calories 292; total fat 8.6 g; cholesterol 26 g; carbohydrates 45.1 g; dietary fiber 3.8 g; protein 7.8 g; sodium 74 mg; potassium 365 mg; calcium 108 mg; iron 1.3 mg; vitamin A 1676 i.u.; vitamin C 81 mg.

SUNSET SIPPER
Per 12-fluid-ounce serving: calories 350; total fat 1.1 g; cholesterol 0 g; carbohydrates 48.7 g; dietary fiber 2.9 g; protein 1.1 g; sodium 3 mg; potassium 330 mg; calcium 24 mg; iron 0.9 mg; vitamin A 57 i.u.; vitamin C 55 mg.

SWEET CHERRY-OT
Per 12-fluid-ounce serving: calories 153; total fat 0.6 g; cholesterol 0 g; carbohydrates 42.9 g; dietary fiber 3.1 g; protein 1.7 g; sodium 3 mg; potassium 312 mg; calcium 57 mg; iron 2 mg; vitamin A 1620 i.u.; vitamin C 30 mg.

TEA-LICIOUS
Per 12-fluid-ounce serving: calories 96; total fat 0.2 g; cholesterol 0 g; carbohydrates 24.2 g; dietary fiber 3.1 g; protein 1.3 g; sodium 2 mg; potassium 269 mg; calcium 49 mg; iron 0.2 mg; vitamin A 273 i.u.; vitamin C 72 mg.

TROPICAL TEASER
Per 12-fluid-ounce serving: calories 274; total fat 3.7 g; cholesterol 0 g; carbohydrates 28.5 g; dietary fiber 2.8 g; protein 1.0 g; sodium 25 mg; potassium 325 mg; calcium 13 mg; iron 0.5 mg; vitamin A 2273 i.u.; vitamin C 31 mg.

UNCANNY CANTALOUPE
Per 12-fluid-ounce serving: calories 251; total fat 3.1 g; cholesterol 7 g; carbohydrates 57 g; dietary fiber 3 g; protein 3.1 g; sodium 52 mg; potassium 628 mg; calcium 67 mg; iron 0.5 mg; vitamin A 3226 i.u.; vitamin C 55 mg.

WATERMELON WAVELENGTH
Per 12-fluid-ounce serving: calories 85; total fat 0.5 g; cholesterol 0 g; carbohydrates 20.9 g; dietary fiber 0.8 g; protein 0.8 g; sodium 74 mg; potassium 149 mg; calcium 12 mg; iron 0.2 mg; vitamin A 441 i.u.; vitamin C 15 mg.

index

107

table of equivalents

The exact equivalents in the following tables have been rounded for convenience.

abbreviations

US/UK	METRIC
oz=ounce	g=gram
lb=pound	kg=kilogram
in=inch	mm=millimeter
ft=foot	cm=centimeter
tbl=tablespoon	ml=milliliter
fl oz=fluid ounce	l=liter
qt=quart	

length measures

⅛ in	3 mm
¼ in	6 mm
½ in	12 mm
1 in	2.5 cm

weights

US/UK	METRIC
1 oz	30 g
2 oz	60 g
3 oz	90 g
4 oz (¼ lb)	125 g
5 oz (⅓ lb)	155 g
6 oz	185 g
7 oz	220 g
8 oz (½ lb)	250 g
10 oz	315 g
12 oz (¾ lb)	375 g
14 oz	440 g
16 oz (1 lb)	500 g
1½ lb	750 g
2 lb	1 kg
3 lb	1.5 kg

liquids

US	METRIC	UK
2 tbl	30 ml	1 fl oz
¼ cup	60 ml	2 fl oz
⅓ cup	80 ml	3 fl oz
½ cup	125 ml	4 fl oz
⅔ cup	160 ml	5 fl oz
¾ cup	180 ml	6 fl oz
1 cup	250 ml	8 fl oz
1½ cups	375 ml	12 fl oz
2 cups	500 ml	16 fl oz